MY LITTLE BOOK OF
ABCs

Illustrations by
Danny Brooks Dalby

Copyright © 2007 Dalmatian Press, LLC. All rights reserved. Printed in the U.S.A.
The DALMATIAN PRESS name and logo are trademarks of Dalmatian Press, LLC, Franklin, Tennessee 37067.
Written permission must be secured from the publisher to use or reproduce any part of this book,
except for brief quotations in critical reviews or publicity.
16309
07 08 09 10 11 NGS 10 9 8 7 6 5 4 3 2 1

A is for *apple*,
shiny and red.

Bb

B is for *blanket*
and boards for
a bed.

Cc

C is for *cat*,
a tabby-striped fellow.

D is for *dog*,
yip-yappy and yellow.

E e

E is for *eagle*
who soars through the sky.

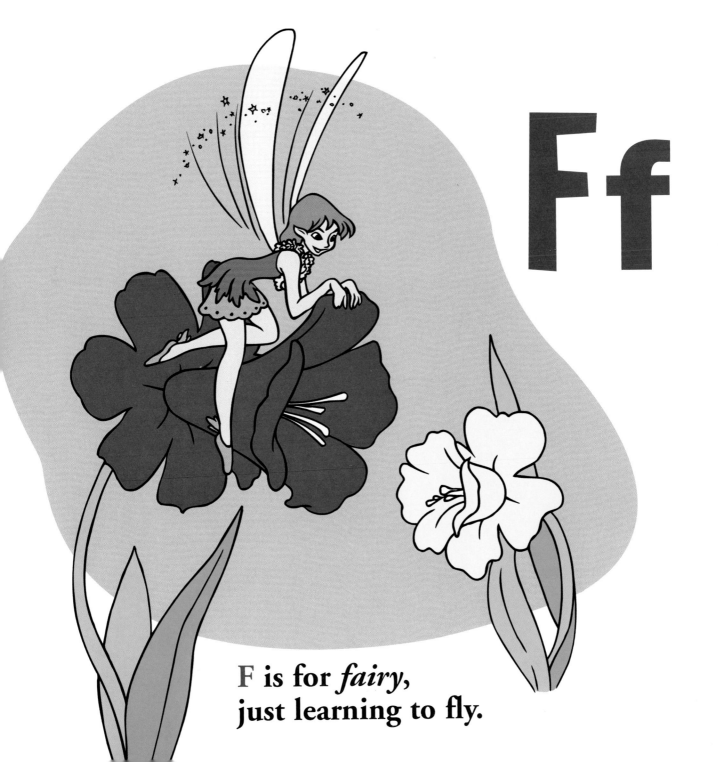

F is for *fairy*,
just learning to fly.

Gg

G is for *garden* that grows in the sun.

H is for *hot dog* to eat on a bun.

I is for *ice cream.*
Do you like strawberry?

J j

J — *Jack-o'-lantern!*
(He's not really scary.)

K is for *kitten*
who's ready to eat.

Ll

L is for *lollipop*,
tasty and sweet.

Mm

M is for *mouse*
in a red, rompy suit.

N is for *nose*.
(And, my—*yours*
is cute!)

Nn

O is for *owl*,
a fellow whoooo's wise.

P is for *pudding*
and peachy-keen pies.

Q is for *quail*
with fluttery
wings.

R is for *rabbit*
and red ruby rings.

S is for *sun*
with a soft, warming glow.

T is for *turtle*
who's taking it s-l-o-w.

U u

U is *umbrella,*
for when the rain comes.

V is for *vacuum*.
Good-bye, dust
and crumbs!

W is for *walrus*
who likes to get wet.

Hello, X, Y, and Z.
Farewell, alphabet!

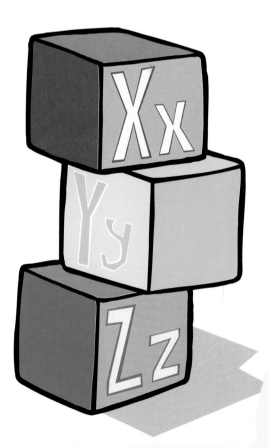